5/22

OPTICAL
ILLUSIONS
to
TRICK THE EYE

Rebecca Felix

Super Sandcastle

An Imprint of Abdo Publishing
abdobooks.com

abdobooks.com

Printed in the United States of America, North Mankato, Minnesota
102019
012020

THIS BOOK CONTAINS
RECYCLED MATERIALS

Design: Aruna Rangarajan, Mighty Media, Inc.
Production: Mighty Media, Inc.
Editor: Rachael Thomas
Design Elements: Shutterstock Images
Cover Photographs: Mighty Media, Inc., Shutterstock Images
Interior Photographs: iStockphoto, p. 6; Mighty Media, Inc., pp. 7, 10, 11, 12, 13, 14, 15,
    16 (project), 17, 18, 19, 20, 21, 23, 24, 25, 26, 27, 28, 29, 30; Shutterstock Images, pp. 4,
    5 (kid), 7 (illusion), 8, 9, 11 (putty, compass), 16, 17 (kid), 20 (kid), 22 (kid), 23 (kid), 25 (kid),
    29 (three kids); Wikimedia Commons, pp. 5, 31
The following manufacturers/names appearing in this book are trademarks: Artist's Loft™,
Elmer's® Glue-All®, Sharpie®

Library of Congress Control Number: 2019943342

Publisher's Cataloging-in-Publication Data
Names: Felix, Rebecca, author.
Title: Optical illusions to trick the eye / by Rebecca Felix
Description: Minneapolis, Minnesota : Abdo Publishing, 2020 | Series: Super simple magic and illusions
Identifiers: ISBN 9781532191602 (lib. bdg.) | ISBN 9781532178337 (ebook)
Subjects: LCSH: Magic tricks--Juvenile literature. | Sleight of hand--Juvenile literature. | Optical illusions--
    Juvenile literature. | Science and magic--Juvenile literature.
Classification: DDC 152.148--dc23

Super SandCastle™ books are created by a team of professional educators, reading specialists, and content developers around five essential components—phonemic awareness, phonics, vocabulary, text comprehension, and fluency—to assist young readers as they develop reading skills and strategies and increase their general knowledge. All books are written, reviewed, and leveled for guided reading and early reading intervention programs for use in shared, guided, and independent reading and writing activities to support a balanced approach to literacy instruction.

To Adult Helpers

The projects in this series are fun and simple. There are just a few things to remember to keep kids safe. Some projects require the use of sharp, hot, or chemical materials. Make sure kids protect their clothes and work surfaces. Review the projects before starting, and be ready to assist when necessary.

Contents

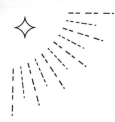

Optical Illusions

Have you ever seen drawings of shapes that appear to spin or flow? Or straight lines that seem to suddenly bend and move? These are optical **illusions**!

ANCIENT AND ASSORTED

In the 1600s, Italian architect Francesco Borromini created an optical illusion at the Palazzo Spada in Rome, Italy. He used angles and columns to make a hallway look much longer than it actually is.

Some optical **illusions** look like two different things at once! Others appear to bend, move, or contain objects that aren't there.

How many **prongs** do you see? Are you sure?

Are these lines straight? Check with a ruler!

Do you see a duck or a rabbit?

Optical **illusions** cause our brains to fill in shapes or movement that aren't really there. So, images look different from how they actually are.

This seems like magic! But like all magic tricks, there are **techniques** and science behind the illusions. With practice, you can create your own optical illusions!

Dutch artist M.C. Escher was famous for his drawings of optical illusions. He created *Day and Night* in 1938.

OPTICAL ILLUSION
Tips and Techniques

It takes careful work to create an optical **illusion**. It is not easy to trick the eyes and brain into seeing things that aren't there. Discover the keys to making this type of magic work!

Details are important to optical **illusions**. How well or exact it is drawn could be the key to making it work. Even the smallest distance between lines or shapes can make a difference! Here are some tips for completing the illusions in this book.

 1 Read the steps carefully.

2 Work slowly.

3 Use exact measurements and suggested colors.

Remember, the brain is smart! Tricking it takes **precision**.

PRACTICE AND PRESENTATION

Even if you've created an **illusion** carefully, it might not work. That's okay! Like all magic tricks, optical illusions take practice. **Presentation** is also important. Don't let your **audience** watch you create the illusion. And, be sure they only see it the correct way.

ILLUSIONIST
Tool Kit

Here are some of the materials that you will need for the tricks in this book.

HOLE PUNCH

CONSTRUCTION PAPER

GLUE

CARD STOCK

PHOTO OF A FACE

TAPE

CLEAR PLASTIC SHEETS

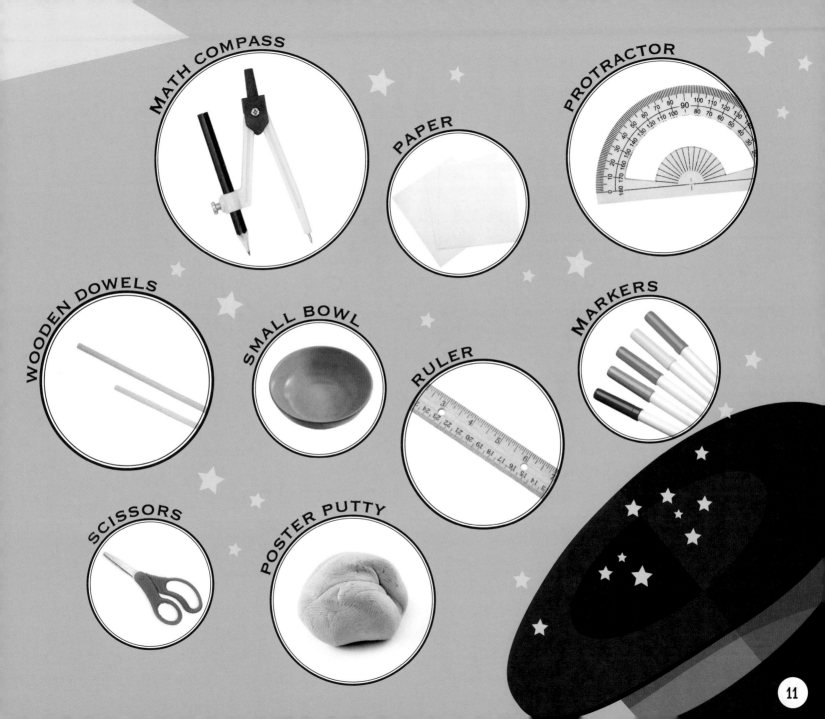

MATH COMPASS

PAPER

PROTRACTOR

WOODEN DOWELS

SMALL BOWL

RULER

MARKERS

SCISSORS

POSTER PUTTY

11

EMOJI AFTERIMAGE

Make two drawings look like one!

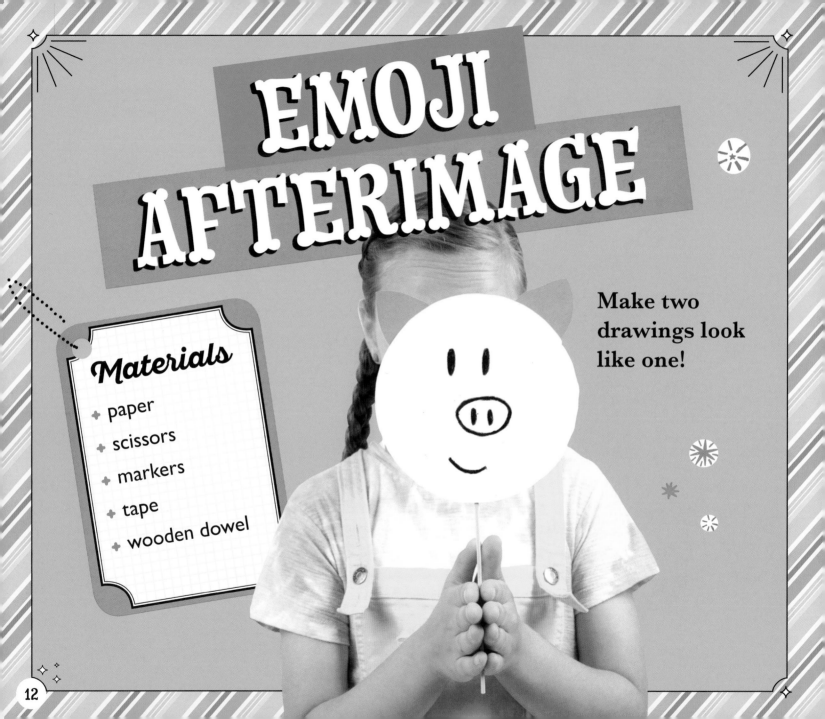

Materials

+ paper
+ scissors
+ markers
+ tape
+ wooden dowel

1 Cut two circles out of paper. Make them the same size. Color one circle pink. Tape on ears.

2 Draw a pig's face in the center of the second paper circle.

3 Set the first circle pink side down on the table. Tape one end of the dowel to the circle.

Amazing

4 Tape the second circle on top so the dowel is between the circles.

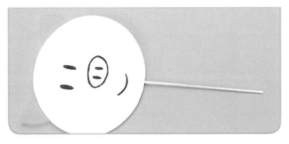

5 Hold the dowel between your hands. Move your hands back and forth to spin the dowel. The pig's features will appear to be on its face! This is an afterimage.

PROP SWAP

+ Swap a stiff straw for the dowel.
+ Think of other image pairs to draw and create afterimages: flower/bee, cloud/bolt of lightning, fishbowl/fish!

FUNNY PHOTO TRICK

Upside down, this warped portrait looks right!

1 Cut the eyes and mouth out of one photo.

2 Turn the eyes cutout upside down. Glue it over the eyes in the full photo.

3 Glue the mouth cutout upside down over the mouth in the full photo.

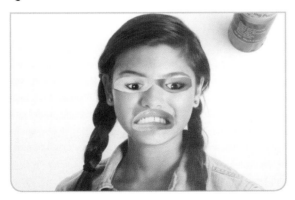

4 Turn the photo upside down. Does it looks normal? Slowly turn the photo right side up to reveal the **illusion**.

BEHIND THE MAGIC

The photo looks normal when upside down because the brain is not used to seeing upside down faces. So, it fills in anything strange with what it expects to see. When the face is right side up, the brain recognizes the oddities!

PUZZLING PARALLELS

Send perfectly parallel lines askew with this simple illusion!

Materials
+ paper
+ marker
+ ruler

1 Use a ruler to draw six angled lines on the paper. Make each line 6 inches (15 cm) long. Space the lines the same distance apart.

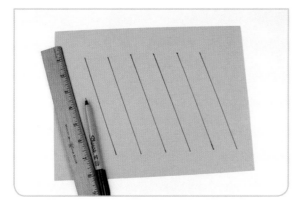

2 Draw dashes across the first, third, and fifth lines. The dashes should be angled so the left ends are higher than the right ends.

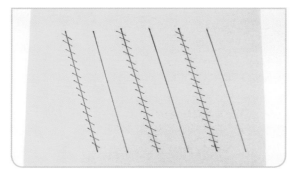

3 Draw dashes across the other three lines. Angle the dashes so the right ends are higher than the left ends.

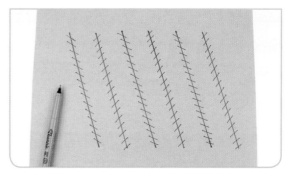

4 Look at the lines. Do they appear to be **parallel**?

Whoa

SEEING CIRCLES

Make a square bend when it meets many circles!

Materials

+ paper
+ ruler
+ scissors
+ marker
+ math compass
+ card stock

1 Cut a 5-inch (13 cm) square out of paper. Use a ruler to find the exact center of the square. Mark the spot with a small dot.

2 Use the compass to draw the smallest circle possible around the dot.

3 Widen the compass by ¼ inch (0.6 cm). Draw a larger circle around the smaller circle.

4 Repeat step 3 until you reach the edges of the paper.

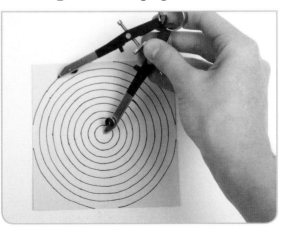

5 Cut a 3-inch (7.5 cm) square out of card stock.

6 Place the square on top of the circles. Make sure it is centered. Trace around the square.

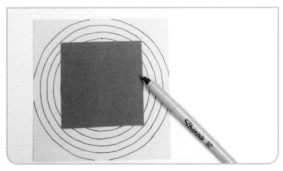

7 Remove the paper square. Look at the drawing. Do the sides of the drawn square look straight?

MAGIC TRIANGLES

Trick an audience into seeing triangles that don't exist!

Materials

+ card stock
+ ruler
+ marker
+ scissors
+ poster putty
+ paper

1 Cut two triangles out of card stock. Make them each 3 inches (7.5 cm) on each side.

2 Use a small piece of poster putty to stick one triangle to a sheet of paper. A corner of the triangle should point up.

3 Stick the other triangle on top of the first, but with a corner pointing down.

4 Trace around each corner of the bottom triangle.

5 Draw a circle over each corner of the top triangle. Color in the circles.

6 Remove the paper triangles. Look at the drawing. Does it appear that the triangles are still there?

PHOTO FRAME MIRAGE

Watch square boxes turn into wavy rows!

Materials

+ white card stock
+ ruler
+ black marker
+ scissors
+ construction paper (black and white)
+ hole punch
+ black marker
+ glue

1 Cut a 7-inch (18 cm) square out of white card stock. Draw a 5-inch (13 cm) square inside it. This makes a frame.

2 Use the ruler to draw a line running down the exact center of each side of the frame.

3 Use the ruler to draw shorter lines dividing the frame into ½-inch (1.25 cm) squares.

4 Color the top left corner square black. Color in every other square on the frame black, so the squares **alternate** between black and white.

5 Number the sides of the frame. The top is 1, the bottom 2, and the left and right sides 3 and 4.

6 Punch 92 white and 92 black dots out of construction paper. The white dots are for the black squares and the black dots are for the white squares.

CONTINUED ON NEXT PAGE

7 Glue a dot to the third white square over from the top left corner of side 1. Glue a dot to the black square below the white square. Place the dots slightly above the center of their squares.

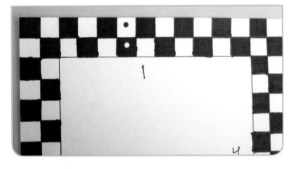

8 Glue dots in the upper left and bottom right corners of the squares to the left of the one-dot squares.

9 Turn the frame so side 2 is at the top. Repeat steps 7 and 8 on side 2.

10 Turn the frame so side 3 is at the top. Glue a dot to the fourth white square over from the top left corner of side 3. Glue a dot to the black square below the white square. Place the dots slightly below the center of their squares.

11 Glue dots in the bottom left and upper right corners of the squares to the left of the one-dot squares.

12 Turn the frame so side 4 is on top. Repeat steps 10 and 11 on side 4.

13 Turn the frame so side 1 is on top. Glue dots in the bottom left and top right corners of the remaining squares on side 1.

14 Turn the frame so side 2 is at the top. Repeat step 13 on side 2.

15 Turn the frame so side 3 is on top. Glue dots in the top left and bottom right corners of the remaining squares on side 3.

16 Turn the frame so side 4 is at the top. Repeat step 15 on side 4.

17 All of the squares should now have dots in them. Do the straight lines look wavy?

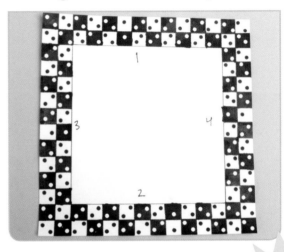

18 Cut the middle square out of the frame. Glue a photo to the back of the frame and display your **illusion**!

Whoa!

MIND-BENDING MOIRÉ SPINNERS

Make patterns that seem to move!

Materials

+ small bowl
+ black permanent marker
+ card stock
+ scissors
+ clear plastic sheets
+ math compass
+ ruler
+ tape

1 Trace the bowl three times on the card stock. Cut out the circles.

2 Trace the bowl three times on the clear plastic. Cut out the circles.

3 Use the compass to draw circles on one of the paper circles.

4 Repeat step 3 on a clear circle. The two circle patterns should be slightly different.

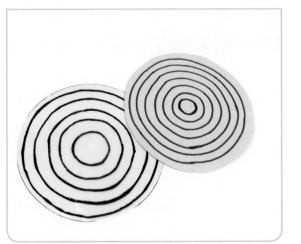

5 Use the ruler to cover another paper circle in a checkerboard pattern.

6 Repeat step 5 on a clear circle. The two checkerboard patterns should be slightly different.

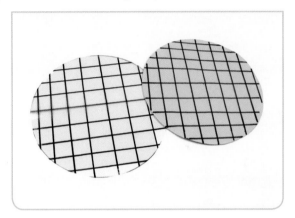

7 Create another pattern on the third paper circle. This could be **diagonal** lines, triangles, or other repeating shapes. Create a pattern that can be repeated easily.

CONTINUED ON NEXT PAGE

8 Draw the same pattern from step 7 on the last clear circle. The two patterns should be slightly different.

9 Fold a small piece of tape over the edge of each circle. The pieces of tape should stick out slightly to form tabs.

10 Place each clear circle on the paper circle with its matching pattern. Use brass fasteners to connect each pair of circles at their centers.

11 Use the tabs to turn the spinners. Do new patterns emerge in a waving motion? These are **moiré** patterns! They are a type of **illusion**.

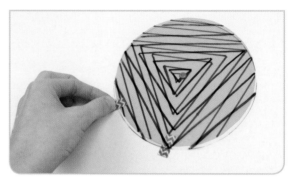

12 Take the spinners apart and combine them in new ways. Move the tabs to see what new illusions appear!

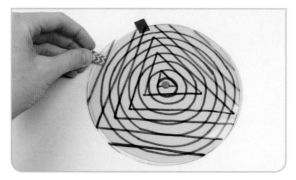

HOST A
MAGIC SHOW!

Magic tricks need more than **props** and practice. They also require an **audience**! When you have a few optical **illusions** ready, put on a magic show for your friends and family. You could try setting up a stage for it. Or, keep it simple and gather your audience around a table.

Cool

Whoa

TIPS TO BECOME A
Master Illusionist

Be **confident** when **presenting** your **illusions**.

Use **props** such as blankets or **scarves** to cover and then reveal each illusion.

Keep an illusion's secret to yourself if you wish. A little mystery makes magic fun!

ICONIC ILLUSIONIST

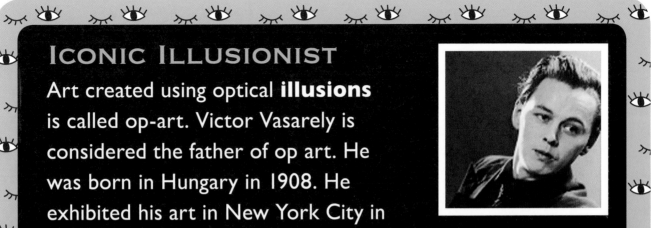

Art created using optical **illusions** is called op-art. Victor Vasarely is considered the father of op art. He was born in Hungary in 1908. He exhibited his art in New York City in 1965. People loved it! Soon after, op art started appearing in advertising, fashion, and product packaging.

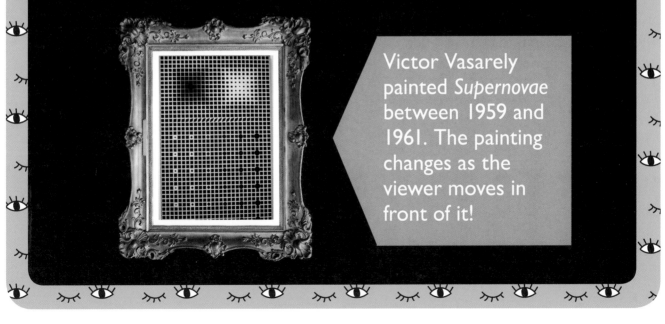

Victor Vasarely painted *Supernovae* between 1959 and 1961. The painting changes as the viewer moves in front of it!

Glossary of Magic Words

alternate – to change back and forth from one to the other.

audience – a group of people watching a performance.

confident – sure of oneself.

diagonal – at an angle.

illusion – something that looks real but is not.

moiré – a wavy or shimmering effect seen when two regular patterns are placed on top of each other at an angle.

parallel – lying or moving in the same direction.

precision – the quality or state of being accurate or exact.

present – to show or talk about something to a group or the public. A performance is called a presentation.

prong – one of the sharp points of a fork, tool, or antler.

prop – an object that is carried or used by a performer in a performance.

scarf – a long piece of cloth worn around the neck for decoration or to keep warm.

technique – a method or style in which something is done.